First published in 2020 by Wide Eyed Editions, an imprint of The Quarto Group.
Quarto Boston North Shore, 100 Cummings Center, Suite 265D, Beverly, MA 01915, USA.
Tel: +1 978-282-9590, Fax: +1 978-283-2742
www.QuartoKnows.com

A catalog record for this book is available from the British Library.

ISBN 978-0-7112-6155-6

The illustrations were created digitally
Set in Lelo
Published by Georgia Amson-Bradshaw
Designed by Zoë Tucker
Production by Dawn Cameron
Manufactured in Guangdong, China EB102020

9 8 7 6 5 4 3 2 1

written by
Zoë Tucker

illustrated by
Mark Wang

WE ARE THE
BEATLES

THE **BEATLES**

WIDE EYED EDITIONS

One day, in the summer of 1957, Paul met up with his friends and went to the local village fair. A new band was playing and he really wanted to hear them.

The band roared
into life.

They were called The Quarrymen and standing at the front, playing guitar and singing, was a 16-year-old boy called John.

They were good!
Toe-tapping and head-boppingly good.
Everyone loved them.

After the concert Paul met John and the two boys talked for hours.

Paul had taught himself to play the guitar, and he played a few songs for John. John thought he sounded pretty good, and asked him to join the band. Paul was excited! He really wanted to impress John.

But at their first concert Paul felt nervous.
He had a big guitar solo, and he wasn't sure
if he would be good enough. Would anyone
like his performance?

He peeped out from the side of the stage and
looked at the crowd. John, who was always
cool as a cucumber, said:

And together,
they stepped out
onto the stage.

Every day after school the two friends raced home to hang out together.

PENNY LANE

John was funny and confident, and Paul was quiet and steady.

John liked poetry and art, Paul liked rock 'n' roll and blues music.

They both loved playing guitar and they spent all their free time writing songs together.

Sometimes they would
hitch-hike to far-off places
just to write new songs.

John would start
a line,

and Paul
would finish it.

John would strum some
chords on his guitar, and Paul
would add the tune.

Sometimes they'd goof around, and sometimes they'd tell each other their deepest hopes and dreams.

The band grew bigger when Paul's friend George joined the group. He was a whizz on the guitar, and he was always introducing the group to new sounds.

But the band grew smaller again when their drummer left.

Over the next couple of years, the band gigged in rowdy London bars,

and performed at weddings . . .

They gained a manager,

and a producer,

and finally, when they found the perfect drummer . . .

John, Paul, George, and Ringo became

The Beatles!

When the Fab Four played together, it was impossible not to like them. They had such a cool sound! They bopped and clapped, they whooped and sang.

THE
BEATLES

People all around the world began to notice them on the radio . . .

. . . and on the television.

Their popularity grew and grew.

The world was changing a lot. The young generation felt inspired and excited by the Beatles' new sound. Who knew what the future might hold?

Before long huge crowds would gather to hear John, Paul, George, and Ringo perform.

Their fans went wild!

They became so popular that in 1965 the Beatles played the first ever stadium concert. 55,000 people arrived to watch them play.

No musicians had ever played to a crowd that big before.

Backstage, the four lads from Liverpool felt really nervous.

John was frightened he might not remember the words.

Ringo worried he'd miss the beat.

They practiced their chords,

and sang their harmonies as they waited to go on.

Then they changed into their suits and ruffled their hair.

The friends looked at one another, and they knew that they could do it. And together, they stepped out onto the stage.

And they were good!
Toe-tapping and head-boppingly good.
Everyone loved them!

Ringo, George, Paul, and John were
each talented in their own way, but together
they were ground-breaking and unique.

The Beatles became the
best band in the world.

WE ARE THE
BEATLES

John Lennon: October 9, 1940 – December 8, 1980

Paul McCartney: June 18, 1942

George Harrison: February 25, 1943 – November 29, 2001

Ringo Starr: July 7, 1940

THE BEATLES rocked the world and changed the music scene forever. Coming together in 1962, John, Paul, George, and Ringo—the four lads from Liverpool—combined their talent and creativity to create a sound that the world had never heard before and in doing so, they inspired an entire generation. The Beatles became the most influential rock band of all time.

At the time, England, like much of Europe and the USA, was still recovering from the Second World War. Times were tough, and people were still feeling sad. The Beatles' music was joyful, happy, and upbeat, and the perfect antidote to the stuffy post-war atmosphere. It was impossible not to love their catchy tunes and four-part harmonies and their songs offered a message of hope at a time when it was most needed.

Before the Beatles came along most musicians performed songs that were written by someone else. The Beatles changed all that. They spent hours jamming in the studio together, often experimenting with unusual instruments and music styles to discover new sounds. Influenced by traditional folk music, rock 'n' roll, blues, and even Classical and Indian music, their work was fresh and new. John and Paul were the songwriting duo at the heart of the band, but each member brought something special to the group.

'Beatlemania' swept the globe. During their eight years together, The Beatles constantly reinvented themselves and were always open to new ideas. They believed people should be able to say and wear whatever they want, which in turn, inspired young people to have fun and be more creative. People wanted to be like the Beatles, to sing and play like the Beatles, and to look like the Beatles. They were worshipped and adored and by 1964 the Beatles were international superstars and mobbed by their fans everywhere they went!

In 1970, the band split up to start solo music careers. After the very intense bond of being in the Beatles, it was a difficult time emotionally and they had falling outs. But after a little while, they became friends again.

The Beatles wrote over 200 songs, they toured the world, sang on TV to millions of people, and starred in movies. Their songs are loved the world over and continue to sell millions of copies. "All You Need is Love" became an anthem for a generation, with a simple but timeless message that still holds true today.